أسئلة وأجوبة للصغار

ولا يستغني عنها الكبار

– الطبعة الثانية –

أسئلة وأجوبة للصغار ولا يستغني عنها الكبار

Q&A for the Young & Indispensable to the Elders

2nd Edition ©Darul Imam Muslim 2017 / 1438

E-mail: contact@darulimammuslim.com

Cover & typesetting by:
Ihsaan Design
www.ihsaandesign.com

Translator's Acknowledgments:
After thanking Allah, I would like to thank the following people for their support and
assistance in publishing this book for the second time: my family – in particular: my
parents and wife, Abu Hurayrah Zulfiker, Abu Abdur-Rahmaan Arif, Umm 'Ubaydillah,
Amatullah, Umm Ibraaheem and 'Abdul-Qaadir; may Allah reward you all with good.

* The Biography of the author on the back cover has been summarised from www.mahad-ul-
furqan.org.

[2ⁿᵈ Edition]

أسئلة وأجوبة للصغار

ولا يستغني عنها الكبار

Questions and Answers for the Young

& Indispensable to the Elders

شيخ سالم بن سعد الطويل

By Shaykh Saalim bin Sa'd at-Taweel

Translated by Abu Faatimah Azhar Majothi

DARUL IMAM MUSLIM

مُقَدِّمَةٌ

Introduction

All the perfect and complete praises are for Allah alone, and may His *salah* and *salam* be on whom there is no Prophet after (i.e. Muhammad ﷺ).

الحمد لله وحده والصلاة والسلام على من لا نبي بعده.

As for what follows: I have prepared these Islamic questions and answers, varying in (matters of) *Aqeedah* (creed), worship, *seerah* (history), manners, etc. for the young to memorise and to aid the elders in teaching their children and students; and that which prompted me to write it was that some of those responsible of the affairs (of education and nurturing) from parents and teachers, were at times uncertain in choosing appropriate questions for children to discuss; so these are the: '*Questions and Answers for the Young, and Indispensable to the Elders.*'

أما بعد: فهذه أسئلة وأجوبة شرعية متنوعة في العقيدة والعبادات والسيرة والآداب ونحوها أعددتما ليحفظها الصغار وليستعين بما الكبار في تعليم أبنائهم وبناتهم وطلاهم وطالباتهم، والذي دعاني إلى كتابتها أن بعض أولياء الأمور من الآباء والأمهات والمدرسين والمدرسات أحيانا يختار في اختيار الأسئلة المناسبة لمحاورة الطفل أو الطفلة، فكانت هذه (الأسئلة والأجوبة للصغار ولا يستغني عنها الكبار).

And I ask Allah that He benefits by it: its reader, memorizer, teacher and student.

والله أسأل أن ينفع بها القارئ والحافظ والمعلم والمتعلم...

Written by one hoping to be pardoned by his *Rabb*:
Saalim bin Sa'd At-Taweel
20th of Rajab 1424 A.H.
Corresponding to 16th September 2003 C.E.
Kuwait

كتبه راجي عفو ربه
سالم بن سعد الطويل ٢٠
رجب ١٤٢٤هـ
الموافق ٢٠٠٣/٩/١٦م
الكويت

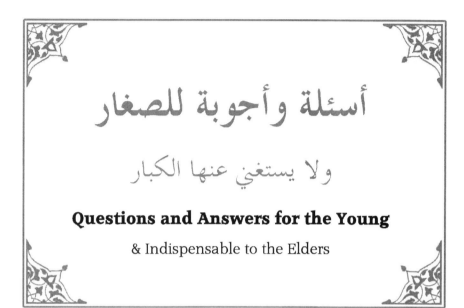

أسئلة وأجوبة للصغار

ولا يستغني عنها الكبار

Questions and Answers for the Young

& Indispensable to the Elders

بِسْمِ اللهِ نَبْدَأُ...

In the Name of Allah, we begin...

1 – Who is your *Rabb*?[1]

Answer: My *Rabb* is Allah the Blessed and Most High.

١ – مَنْ رَبُّكَ؟

الْجَوَابُ: رَبِّيَ اللهُ تَبَارَكَ وَتَعَالَى.

---

[1] [TN] *Ar-Rabb* (الرب) means: the Creator and Owner of all things, and the Controller of every affair; it is also one of the Names of Allah ﷻ.

2 – Where is Allah the Blessed and Most High?
Answer: Allah the Most High is above the Heavens.

٢ – أَيْنَ اللهُ تَبَارَكَ وَتَعَالَى؟

الْجَوَابُ: اللهُ تَعَالَى فِي السَّمَاءِ.

3 – What is Allah's Right over His slaves?
Answer: That they worship Him (alone) and do not do make any partners with Him (in worship).

٣ – مَا حَقُّ اللهِ عَلَى الْعِبَادِ؟

الْجَوَابُ: أَنْ يَعْبُدُوهُ وَلَا يُشْرِكُوا بِهِ شَيْئًا.

4 – Complete the (following) *Hadeeth*: The Messenger of Allah ﷺ said: "*Whoever says: 'I am pleased with Allah as my Rabb...*"?
Answer: "*...and with Islam as my Deen*[2] *and with Muhammad* ﷺ *as my Prophet, (then) Jannah becomes obligatory for him.*"[3]

٤ – أَكْمِلِ الْحَدِيثَ... قَال رَسُولُ اللهِ ﷺ: ((مَنْ قَال رَضِيتُ بِاللهِ رَبًّا...؟

الْجَوَابُ: ...وَبِالإِسْلام دِينًا وَبِمُحَمَّدٍ صَلَّى اللهُ عَلَيْهِ وَسَلَّمَ نَبِيًّا وَجَبَتْ لَهُ الْجَنَّةُ)).

5 – Why did Allah the Most High create us? And what is the evidence?
Answer: To worship Him alone; He the Most High said: ⟨*And I did not create the jinn or mankind except to worship Me (alone).*⟩[4]

٥ – لِمَاذَا خَلَقَنَا اللهُ تَعَالَى؟ وَمَا الدَّلِيلُ؟

الْجَوَابُ: لِعِبَادَتِهِ وَحْدَهُ، قَال تَعَالَى: ﴿ وَمَا خَلَقْتُ الْجِنَّ وَالإِنسَ إِلَّا لِيَعْبُدُونِ ﴾.

---

[2] [TN] *Deen*: A religion or system which a person submits to and obeys. The *Deen* of Islam is the religion and system which includes everything that Allah sent the Messenger of Allah ﷺ with, from rulings, laws, matters of creed etc., including statements and actions.
[3] Recorded by Aboo Daawood (1529) from Aboo Sa'eed Al-Khudri ؓ.
[4] Adh-Dhaariyat (51):56.

6 – What is the greatest obligation upon us?
Answer: *At-Tawheed* and it is to single out Allah the Most High with all that He deserves.[5]

٦- مَا أَعْظَمُ وَاجِبٍ عَلَيْنَا؟
الْجَوَابُ: التَّوْحِيدُ، وَهُوَ إِفْرَادُ اللهِ تَعَالَى بِمَا يَسْتَحِقُّ.

7 – Mention the types of *Tawheed?*
Answer: *Tawheed-ur-Ruboobiyyah*[6], *Tawheed-ul-Uloohiyyah*[7] and *Tawheed-ul-Asmaa'i was-Sifaat*[8].

٧- أُذْكُرْ أَنْوَاعَ التَّوْحِيدِ؟
الْجَوَابُ: تَوْحِيدُ الرُّبُوبِيَّةِ وَتَوْحِيدُ الأُلُوهِيَّةِ وَتَوْحِيدُ الأَسْمَاءِ وَالصِّفَاتِ.

8 – What is the *Kalimat-ut-Tawheed?* And what is its meaning?
Answer: The *Kalimat-ut-Tawheed* is: '*laa ilaaha illallah*' and its meaning is: there is nothing truly deserving of worship except Allah (alone).

٨- مَا كَلِمَةُ التَّوْحِيدِ؟ وَمَا مَعْنَاهَا؟
الْجَوَابُ: كَلِمَةُ التَّوْحِيدِ هِيَ: لا إِلَهَ إلاّ اللهُ، وَمَعْنَاهَا: لا مَعْبُودَ حَقٌّ إلا اللهُ.

9 – Complete the (following) *Hadeeth*: The Messenger of Allah ﷺ said: "*There is nobody who testifies that there is nothing deserving of*

٩- أَكْمِلِ الْحَدِيثَ... قَال رَسُولُ اللهِ ﷺ: ((مَا مِنْ أَحَدٍ يَشْهَدُ أَنْ لا إِلَهَ إلاّ اللهُ

---

[5] [TN] i.e. to single Him out in His *ar-Ruboobiyyah, al-Uloohiyyah and al-Asmaa'u was-Sifaat*. See question 7.
[6] [TN] *Tawheed-ur-Ruboobiyyah* is to single out Allah in His actions, like creating, sustaining, causing life and death, etc.
[7] [TN] *Tawheed-ul-Uloohiyyah* is to single out Allah in all acts of worship, like prayer, fasting, *Hajj, Zakaah*, making oaths, sacrificing animals, etc.
[8] [TN] *Tawheed-ul-Asmaa'i was-Sifaat* is to describe Allah according to how He and his Messenger Muhammad ﷺ described Him, and to refer to Him by the Names He and His Messenger ﷺ referred to Him with, all of which must be done without comparing (*tashbeeh*) or likening (*tamtheel*) Allah to the creation, nor altering their meanings (*tahreef*) or denying their reality (*ta'teel*). See '*The Correct Islaamic Aqeedah*' by Shaykh Bin Baaz, Daar us-Sunnah Publications.

worship except Allah (alone) and that Muhammad is indeed the Messenger of Allah..."?

وَأَنَّ مُحَمَّدًا رَسُولُ اللهِ...؟

Answer: "...truthfully from his heart, except that Allah makes the Fire (of Hell) forbidden for him.[9]

الْجَوَابُ: ...صِدْقًا مِنْ قَلْبِهِ إِلاَّ حَرَّمَهُ اللهُ عَلَى النَّارِ)).

10 – What is the greatest of sins?

١٠ – مَا أَعْظَمُ الذُّنُوبِ؟

Answer: Shirk[10] with Allah.

الْجَوَابُ: الشِّرْكُ بِاللهِ.

11 – What is Shirk?

١١ – مَا الشِّرْكُ؟

Answer: It is worshipping an ilaah[11] instead of Allah or (worshipping it) along with Allah the Most High.

الْجَوَابُ: هُوَ عِبَادَةُ إِلهٍ مِنْ دُونِ اللهِ تَعَالَى أَوْ مَعَ اللهِ تَعَالَى.

12 – Complete the (following) Hadeeth: The Messenger of Allah 🕮 said: "Whoever swears an oath by other than Allah..."?

١٢ – أَكْمِلِ الْحَدِيثَ... قَالَ رَسُولُ اللهِ 🕮: ((مَنْ حَلَفَ بِغَيْرِ اللهِ...؟

Answer: "...then he has committed disbelief or Shirk."[12]

الْجَوَابُ: ...فَقَدْ كَفَرَ أَوْ أَشْرَكَ)).

13 – Does anyone know the Unseen other than Allah?

١٣ – هَلْ يَعْلَمُ أَحَدٌ الْغَيْبَ سِوَى اللهِ؟

---

[9] Recorded by Al-Bukhaaree (128) and Muslim (32) from Anas bin Maalik 🕭.

[10] [TN] See question 11.

[11] [TN] An ilaah is anything that is taken as something deserving of worship, love and obedience, or sought as a giver of benefit and protector from harm.

[12] Recorded by At-Tirmidhee (1535) from ('Abdullah) Ibn 'Umar 🕭.

TN: Shaykh Al-Albaanee graded it Saheeh.

Answer: ❨*Nobody in the heavens or earth knows the Unseen other than Allah* (Who is above the heavens).❩[13]

الْجَوَابُ: ﴿لَّا يَعْلَمُ مَن فِى ٱلسَّمَـٰوَٰتِ وَٱلْأَرْضِ ٱلْغَيْبَ إِلَّا ٱللَّهُ﴾.

14 – When are actions accepted by Allah the Most High?

١٤- مَتَى تَكُونُ الْأَعْمَالُ مَقْبُولَةً عِنْدَ الله تَعَالَى؟

Answer: When they are (done) sincerely for Allah the Most High and in agreement with the *Sunnah* of the Messenger of Allah ﷺ.

الْجَوَابُ: إِذَا كَانَتْ خَالِصَةً لله تَعَالَى وَمُوَافِقَةً لِسُنَّةِ رَسُولِ الله ﷺ.

15 – Recite *Surat-ul-Kaafiroon*?

١٥- اقْرَأْ سُورَةَ الْكَافِرُونَ؟

Answer:[14]

الْجَوَابُ:

بِسْمِ اللَّهِ الرَّحْمَٰنِ الرَّحِيمِ

﴿قُلْ يَـٰٓأَيُّهَا ٱلْكَـٰفِرُونَ . لَآ أَعْبُدُ مَا تَعْبُدُونَ . وَلَآ أَنتُمْ عَـٰبِدُونَ مَآ أَعْبُدُ وَلَآ أَنَا۠ عَابِدٌ مَّا عَبَدتُّمْ . وَلَآ أَنتُمْ عَـٰبِدُونَ مَآ أَعْبُدُ . لَكُمْ دِينُكُمْ وَلِىَ دِينِ﴾

(In the Name of Allah Ar-Rahmaan Ar-Raheem) "(1) Say: 'O you disbelievers! (2) I do not worship that which you worship, (3) And you are not worshippers of that which I worship, (4) And I am not a worshipper of what you are worshipping, (5) And you are not worshippers of that which I worship, (6) To you be your deen, and to me my Deen (i.e. Islam).'"

16 – Who is your Prophet?

١٦- مَنْ نَبِيُّكَ؟

Answer: Muhammad, the Messenger of Allah ﷺ.

الْجَوَابُ: مُحَمَّدٌ رَسُولُ الله ﷺ.

---

[13] An-Naml (27):65
[14] Al-Kaafiroon (109):1-6

17 – What is the meaning of 'Muhammad is the Messenger of Allah' ?
Answer: It means: Allah the Most High sent him (ﷺ) to the whole of mankind as a giver of good news and as a warner.

١٧ – مَا مَعْنَى مُحَمَّدٌ رَسُولُ اللهِ ﷺ؟

الْجَوَابُ: أَيْ أَرْسَلَهُ اللهُ تَعَالَى لِلنَّاسِ كَافَّةً بَشِيرًا وَنَذِيرًا.

18 – What is the name of our Prophet ﷺ and the name of his father and his grandfather?
Answer: Muhammad (ﷺ), the son of 'Abdullah, the son of 'Abdul-Muttalib.

١٨ – مَا اسْمُ نَبِيِّنَا ﷺ وَاسْمُ أَبِيهِ وَاسْمُ جَدِّهِ؟

الْجَوَابُ: مُحَمَّدُ بْنُ عَبْدِاللهِ بْنِ عَبْدِالْمُطَّلِبِ.

19 – Who is it obligatory for you to love the most out of all mankind?

Answer: The Messenger of Allah ﷺ.

١٩ – مَنْ يَجِبُ أَنْ تُحِبَّ أَكْثَرَ مِنْ جَمِيعِ النَّاسِ؟

الْجَوَابُ: رَسُولُ اللهِ ﷺ.

20 – When was the Prophet ﷺ born and in which city?
Answer: In the *Year of the Elephant*[15] in (the city of) Makkah.

٢٠ – مَتَى وُلِدَ النَّبِيُّ ﷺ وَ فِي أَيِّ بَلَدٍ؟

الْجَوَابُ: فِي عَامِ الْفِيلِ بِمَكَّةَ.

21 – How old was the Prophet ﷺ when Allah the Most High sent him

٢١ – كَمْ سَنَةً كَانَ عُمُرُ النَّبِيِّ ﷺ لَمَّا

---

(15) [TN] The *Year of the Elephant* is the year in which the Abyssinian army of Abrahah, which included elephants, failed in their attempt to conquer Makkah and destroy the *Ka'bah*; Allah ﷺ destroyed them by sending against them birds who pelted them with stones of baked clay, as mentioned in *Soorat-ul-Feel* (105):1-5. See '*When the Moon Split*' by S. Mubarakpuri, Darussalam.

(with the message of Islam)?

Answer: Forty years.

أَرْسَلَهُ اللهُ تَعَالَى؟

الْجَوَابُ: أَرْبَعُونَ سَنَةً.

22 – How many years did the
Prophet ﷺ live in Makkah after the
Prophet-hood and before the
hijrah[16]?

Answer: Thirteen years.

٢٢ – كَمْ سَنَةً عَاشَ النَّبِيُّ ﷺ فِي مَكَّةَ بَعْدَ
النُّبُوَّةِ وَقَبْلَ الْهِجْرَةِ؟

الْجَوَابُ: ثَلَاثَ عَشْرَةَ سَنَةً.

23 – Where did the Prophet ﷺ
make *hijrah* to?

Answer: To Madeenah.

٢٣ – إِلَى أَيْنَ هَاجَرَ النَّبِيُّ ﷺ؟

الْجَوَابُ: إِلَى الْمَدِينَةِ.

24 – How many years did the
Prophet ﷺ live in Madeenah after
the *hijrah*?

Answer: Ten years.

٢٤ – كَمْ سَنَةً عَاشَ النَّبِيُّ ﷺ فِي الْمَدِينَةِ
بَعْدَ الْهِجْرَةِ؟

الْجَوَابُ: عَشْرَ سَنَوَاتٍ.

25 – Who are the '*Mothers of the
Believers*' (ﷺ)?

Answer: The wives of the Prophet ﷺ.

٢٥ – مَنْ هُنَّ أُمَّهَاتُ الْمُؤْمِنِينَ؟

الْجَوَابُ: زَوْجَاتُ النَّبِيِّ ﷺ.

26 – Where did the Prophet ﷺ die?
And when? And how old was he?

Answer: In Madeenah, ten years after
the *hijrah* and his age was sixty-three.

٢٦ – أَيْنَ تُوُفِّيَ النَّبِيُّ ﷺ؟ وَمَتَى؟ وَكَمْ
كَانَ عُمُرُهُ؟

الْجَوَابُ: فِي الْمَدِينَةِ بَعْدَ الْهِجْرَةِ بِعَشْرِ
سَنَوَاتٍ، وَكَانَ عُمُرُهُ ثَلَاثًا وَسِتِّينَ سَنَةً.

---

[16] [TN] *Hijrah* (migration) in this context refers to the migration which the Messenger of Allah
ﷺ and his companions ؓ made from Makkah to Madeenah. In its general meaning, it refers to
migrating from the land of *shirk* to the land of *Islaam*.

27 – Complete the (following) *Hadeeth*: The Messenger of Allah ﷺ said: "*Whoever sends salaah*[17] *upon me once...*"?
Answer: "*...Allah will send salaah*[18] *upon him ten times."*[19]

٢٧ – أَكْمِلِ الْحَدِيثَ... قَالَ رَسُولُ اللهِ ﷺ: ((مَنْ صَلَّى عَلَيَّ وَاحِدَةً...؟
الْجَوَابُ: صَلَّى اللهُ عَلَيْهِ بِهَا عَشْرًا)).

28 – What is your *Deen*?
Answer: My *Deen* is al-Islam.

٢٨ – مَا دِينُكَ؟
الْجَوَابُ: دِينِي الْإِسْلَامُ.

29 - What is the meaning of Islam?
Answer: Submission and compliance to Allah by worship and obedience.

٢٩ – مَا مَعْنَى الْإِسْلَامِ؟
الْجَوَابُ: الِاسْتِسْلَامُ وَالِانْقِيَادُ للهِ بِالْعِبَادَةِ وَالطَّاعَةِ.

30 – How many pillars are there in Islam?
Answer: Five pillars.

٣٠ – كَمْ أَرْكَانُ الْإِسْلَامِ؟
الْجَوَابُ: خَمْسَةُ أَرْكَانٍ.

31 – Complete the (following) *Hadeeth*.
The Messenger of Allah ﷺ said: "*Islam is built on five:...*"
Answer: "*...(1) the testification that there is nothing deserving of worship except Allah (alone) and that*

٣١ – أَكْمِلِ الْحَدِيثَ... قَالَ رَسُولُ اللهِ ﷺ: ((بُنِيَ الْإِسْلَامُ عَلَى خَمْسٍ:...؟
الْجَوَابُ: ...شَهَادَةِ أَنْ لَا إِلٰهَ إِلَّا اللهُ وَأَنَّ

---

[17] [TN] Sending *Salaah* upon the Messenger of Allah ﷺ is a *dua'* to Allah, asking Him to mention, praise and honour Muhammad (ﷺ) in the highest gathering in which the best of Angels congregate.
[18] [TN] Allah sending *Salaah* upon a Muslim means His praising him in the highest gathering in which the best of Angels congregate.
[19] Recorded by Muslim (408) from Abu Hurayrah ﷺ.

Muhammad is indeed the Messenger of Allah (ﷺ), *(2) And establishing the Salaah correctly, (3) And giving the Zakaah, (4) And Hajj (5) and fasting Ramadaan.*"[20]

مُحَمَّدًا رَسُولُ اللهِ، وَإِقَامَ الصَّلَاةِ، وَإِيتَاءِ الزَّكَاةِ، وَالْحَجِّ، وَصَوْمُ رَمَضَانَ)).

32 – What is the supporting pillar[21] of Islam?
Answer: The *Salaah.*

٣٢- مَا عُمُودُ الإِسْلَامِ؟
الْجَوَابُ: الصَّلَاةُ.

33 – Complete the (following) *Hadeeth*: The Messenger of Allah ﷺ said: "*The ahd (covenant which differentiates) between us and them (the disbelievers) is the Salaah,…*"?
Answer: "*…so whoever leaves it then he has disbelieved.*"[22]

٣٣- أَكْمِلِ الْحَدِيثَ... قَالَ رَسُولُ اللهِ ﷺ: ((الْعَهْدُ الَّذِي بَيْنَنَا وَبَيْنَهُمْ الصَّلَاةُ...؟
الْجَوَابُ: ...فَمَنْ تَرَكَهَا فَقَدْ كَفَرَ)).

34 – Define the *Salaah?*

Answer: The *Salaah* is worship to Allah with specific statements and actions; it is begun with the *Takbeer*[23] and completed with the *Tasleem*[24].

٣٤- عَرِّفِ الصَّلَاةَ؟
الْجَوَابُ: الصَّلَاةُ هِيَ التَّعَبُّدُ للهِ بِأَقْوَالٍ وَأَفْعَالٍ مَخْصُوصَةٍ مُفْتَتَحَةٍ بِالتَّكْبِيرِ وَمُخْتَتَمَةٍ بِالتَّسْلِيمِ.

35 – How many *Salaahs* are obligatory upon the Muslim during the day and night? And what is the

٣٥- كَمْ صَلَاةً تَجِبُ عَلَى الْمُسْلِمِ فِي الْيَوْمِ وَاللَّيْلَةِ؟ وَكَمْ عَدَدُ رَكَعَاتِهَا؟

---

[20] Recorded by Al-Bukhaaree (8) [and the wording is his] and Muslim (16) from Ibn 'Umar ﷺ.

[21] [TN] i.e. the supporting pillar without which Islaam cannot be established.

[22] Recorded by At-Tirmidhee (2621) and Ibn Maajah (1079) from Buraydah ﷺ. ([TN] Shaykh Al-Albaanee graded it *Saheeh*.)

[23] [TN] The statement: "*Allahu Akbar*" (Allah is the Most Great).

[24] [TN] The statement: "*Assalaamu 'alaikum wa Rahmatullah*" (may Allah's peace and mercy by upon you).

number of their *Rak'aat*?

Answer: There are five *Salaahs*:

الْجَوَابُ: خَمْسُ صَلَوَاتٍ:

1) *Salaat-ul-Fajr* (two *rak'aat*)

(١) صَلَاةُ الْفَجْرِ (رَكْعَتَانِ).

2) *Salaat-ul-Thuhr* (four *rak'aat*).

(٢) صَلَاةُ الظُّهْرِ (أَرْبَعُ رَكَعَاتٍ).

3) *Salaat-ul 'Asr* (four *rak'aat*).

(٣) صَلَاةُ الْعَصْرِ (أَرْبَعُ رَكَعَاتٍ).

4) *Salaat- ul- Maghrib* (three *rak'aat*).

(٤) صَلَاةُ الْمَغْرِبِ (ثَلَاثُ رَكَعَاتٍ).

5) *Salaat-ul 'Ishaa'i* (four *rak'aat*).

(٥) صَلَاةُ الْعِشَاءِ (أَرْبَعُ رَكَعَاتٍ).

36 – What are the conditions of *Salah*?

٣٦ – مَا شُرُوطُ الصَّلَاةِ؟

Answer: The conditions are:

الْجَوَابُ: الشُّرُوطُ هِيَ:

1) Islam.

(١) الْإِسْلَامُ.

2) A sound mind.

(٢) الْعَقْلُ.

3) The age of *tamyeez*.[25]

(٣) التَّمْيِيزُ.

4) The entering of the time (of *Salaah*).

(٤) دُخُولُ الْوَقْتِ.

5) The removal of any impurities.

(٥) إِزَالَةُ النَّجَاسَةِ.

6) Purity (*Wudhu'*).

(٦) الطَّهَارَةُ.

7) Covering the *awrah*.[26]

(٧) سَتْرُ الْعَوْرَةِ.

8) Facing the *Qiblah*.[27]

(٨) اِسْتِقْبَالُ الْقِبْلَةِ.

9) The Intention.

(٩) النِّيَّةُ.

37 – What are the pillars of *Wudoo'u*?

٣٧ – مَا أَرْكَانُ الْوُضُوءِ؟

---

[25] [TN] *Tamyeez*: the stage of later childhood which is realized at the age of seven.

[26] [TN] The *'awrah* is the area of the body which a Muslim is required to cover.

[27] [TN] The direction of the *Qiblah* is the Ka'bah, in *Masjid-ul-Haraam*, Makkah.

Answer:

1) Washing the face, including the *madmadah* and *istinshaaq*.[28]

2) Washing the two hands up-to and including the elbows.

3) Wiping the head including the two ears.

4) Washing the two feet including the heels.

5) Doing the actions in order.

6) Doing the actions consecutively.

38 – What are the nullifiers of *Wudoo'u*?

Answer:

1) Something exiting the two pathways, like urine, excrement, and wind.

2) Sleep.

3) Eating camel meat.

4) Anything which requires a bath (*ghusl*).

39 – Complete the (following) *Hadeeth*: The Messenger of Allah ﷺ said: "*Whoever makes Wudhoo', then says: 'I testify that there is nothing deserving of worship except Allah,*

الْجَوَابُ:

(١) غَسْلُ الْوَجْهِ مَعَ الْمَضْمَضَةِ وَالاسْتِنْشَاقِ.

(٢) غَسْلُ الْيَدَيْنِ مَعَ الْمِرْفَقَيْنِ.

(٣) مَسْحُ الرَّأْسِ مَعَ الأُذُنَيْنِ.

(٤) غَسْلُ الرِّجْلَيْنِ مَعَ الْكَعْبَيْنِ.

(٥) التَّرْتِيبُ.

(٦) الْمُوَالاةُ.

٣٨ – مَا نَوَاقِضُ الْوُضُوءِ؟

الْجَوَابُ:

(١) الْخَارِجُ مِنَ السَّبِيلَيْنِ كَالْبَوْلِ وَالْغَائِطِ وَالرِّيحِ.

(٢) النَّوْمُ.

(٣) أَكْلُ لَحْمِ الإِبْلِ.

(٤) مُوجِبَاتُ الْغُسْلِ.

٣٩ – أَكْمِلِ الْحَدِيثَ... قَالَ رَسُولُ اللهِ ﷺ: ((مَنْ تَوَضَّأَ فَقَالَ: أَشْهَدُ أَنْ لا إِلهَ إِلاَّ اللهُ وَحْدَهُ لا شَرِيكَ لَهُ...))؟

---

[28] [TN] The *madmadah* means to wash one's mouth with water and *istinshaaq* means to sniff water into the nose and blow it out.

Him alone, He has no partners..."?

Answer: "*...And I testify (that) indeed Muhammad (ﷺ) is His slave and His Messenger', the eight gates of Jannah open for him, he may enter (it) from whichever one he wishes.*"[29]

40 – What recitation is obligatory in the *Salaah*?

Answer: *Surat-ul-Faatihah.*

41 – What does the one praying *Salaah* say in *Rukoo*?

Answer: (He says) "*My Rabb the Great is free from all types of imperfections.*"

42 – What does the one praying *Salaah* say during *Sujood*?

Answer: (He says) "*My Rabb the Most High is free from all types of imperfections.*"

43 – What does the one praying *Salaah* say between the two *Sujoods*?

Answer: (He says) "*My Rabb, forgive me; My Rabb, forgive me.*"

44 – Recite the *At-Tahiyyaat*?

Answer: "*All words of glorification are for Allah, and (so are all) prayers, and pure statements and actions; Peace be upon you O Prophet (ﷺ) and mercy of*

الْجَوَابُ: وَأَشْهَدُ أَنَّ مُحَمَّدًا عَبْدُهُ وَرَسُولُهُ، فُتِحَتْ لَهُ أَبْوَابُ الْجَنَّةِ الثَّمَانِيَةُ يَدْخُلُ مِنْ أَيِّهَا شَاءَ)).

٤٠ – مَا الْوَاجِبُ قِرَاءَتُهُ فِي الصَّلَاةِ؟

الْجَوَابُ: سُورَةُ الْفَاتِحَةِ.

٤١ – مَاذَا يَقُولُ الْمُصَلِّي فِي الرُّكُوعِ؟

الْجَوَابُ: سُبْحَانَ رَبِّيَ الْعَظِيمِ.

٤٢ – مَاذَا يَقُولُ الْمُصَلِّي فِي السُّجُودِ؟

الْجَوَابُ: سُبْحَانَ رَبِّيَ الأَعْلَى.

٤٣ – مَاذَا يَقُولُ الْمُصَلِّي بَيْنَ السَّجْدَتَيْنِ؟

الْجَوَابُ: رَبِّ اغْفِرْ لِي، رَبِّ اغْفِرْ لِي.

٤٤ – اِقْرَأْ التَّحِيَّاتِ؟

الْجَوَابُ: التَّحِيَّاتُ لله وَالصَّلَوَاتُ وَالطَّيِّبَاتُ، السَّلَامُ عَلَيْكَ أَيُّهَا النَّبِيُّ وَرَحْمَةُ الله

Allah and His blessings; Peace be upon us and upon the righteous slaves; And I testify that there is nothing deserving of worship except Allah, and that Muhammad (ﷺ) is His slave and His Messenger."[30]

وَبَرَكَاتُهُ، السَّلَامُ عَلَيْنَا وَعَلَى عِبَادِ اللهِ الصَّالِحِينَ، أَشْهَدُ أَنْ لَا إِلَهَ إِلاَّ اللهُ وَأَشْهَدُ أَنَّ مُحَمَّدًا عَبْدُهُ وَرَسُولُهُ.

45 – Recite the *Salaat-ul-Ibraaheemiyyah*?

Answer: *"O Allah send salaah upon Muhammad and upon the aal*[31] *of Muhammad just as You sent praise upon Ibraaheem and the aal of Ibraaheem, indeed You are the Praiseworthy, the Magnificent; and send Your blessings upon Muhammad and upon the aal of Muhammad just as You sent Your blessings upon Ibraaheem and upon the aal of Ibraaheem, indeed You are the Praiseworthy, the Magnificent."*

٤٥ - اِقْرَأْ الصَّلَاةَ الإِبْرَاهِيمِيَّةَ؟

الْجَوَابُ: اللَّهُمَّ صَلِّ عَلَى مُحَمَّدٍ وَعَلَى آلِ مُحَمَّدٍ كَمَا صَلَّيْتَ عَلَى إِبْرَاهِيمَ وَعَلَى آلِ إِبْرَاهِيمَ، إِنَّكَ حَمِيدٌ مَجِيدٌ، وَبَارِكْ عَلَى مُحَمَّدٍ وَعَلَى آلِ مُحَمَّدٍ كَمَا بَارَكْتَ عَلَى إِبْرَاهِيمَ وَعَلَى آلِ إِبْرَاهِيمَ، إِنَّكَ حَمِيدٌ مَجِيدٌ.

46 – What are the four things which the one praying *Salaah* seeks protection with Allah from before the *Tasleem*?

Answer: He says: *"O Allah, I seek protection with You from the punishment of Jahannam (the Hellfire); and from the punishment of the grave and from the trial of life and death; and from the trial of the (false) Messiah: the*

٤٦ - مَا الأَرْبَعُ الَّتِي يَسْتَعِيذُ الْمُصَلِّي بِاللهِ مِنْهَا قَبْلَ التَّسْلِيمِ؟

الْجَوَابُ: يَقُولُ: ((اللَّهُمَّ إِنِّي أَعُوذُ بِكَ مِنْ عَذَابِ جَهَنَّمَ، وَمِنْ عَذَابِ الْقَبْرِ، وَمِنْ فِتْنَةِ الْمَحْيَا وَالْمَمَاتِ، وَمِنْ فِتْنَةِ الْمَسِيحِ

---

[30] Recorded by Al-Bukhaaree (6230) and Muslim (402) from 'Abdullah bin Mas'ood ﷺ.

[31] [TN] *Aal* may refer to the family of the Prophet ﷺ who believed in him or all those who believed and followed him.

Dajjaal."[32]

((الدَّجَّال)).

47 – Complete the (following) *Hadeeth*: The Messenger of Allah ﷺ said: "*Whoever (regularly) prays twelve voluntary rak'aat to Allah...*"

Answer: "*...Allah builds for him a house in Jannah.*"[33]

٤٧ – أَكْمِلِ الْحَدِيثَ... قَالَ رَسُولُ اللهِ ﷺ: ((مَنْ صَلَّى للهِ اثْنَتَيْ عَشْرَةَ رَكْعَةً تَطَوُّعًا...؟

الْجَوَابُ: ...بَنَى اللهُ لَهُ بَيْتًا فِي الْجَنَّةِ)).

48 – Mention the *Sunnah* and *Rawaatib* prayers?[34]

Answer:

1) Two *Rak'aat* before *Fajr (Salaah)*.

2) Four *Rak'aat* before *Thuhr (Salaah)*.

3) Two *Rak'aat* after *Thuhr (Salaah)*.

4) Two *Rak'aat* after *Maghrib (Salaah)*.

5) Two *Rak'aat* after *'Ishaa'a (Salaah)*.

٤٨ – اذْكُرِ السُّنَنَ وَالرَّوَاتِبَ؟

الْجَوَابُ:

(١) رَكْعَتَانِ قَبْلَ الْفَجْرِ.

(٢) أَرْبَعُ رَكَعَاتٍ قَبْلَ الظُّهْرِ.

(٣) رَكْعَتَانِ بَعْدَ الظُّهْرِ.

(٤) رَكْعَتَانِ بَعْدَ الْمَغْرِبِ.

(٥) رَكْعَتَانِ بَعْدَ الْعِشَاءِ.

49 – Define *Zakaah*?

Answer: It is a compulsory right on a specific amount of wealth (that if a Muslim owns, then he must give it) to a specific group[35] at a specific time.

٤٩ – عَرِّفِ الزَّكَاةَ؟

الْجَوَابُ: هِيَ حَقٌّ وَاجِبٌ فِي مَالٍ خَاصٍّ لِطَائِفَةٍ مَخْصُوصَةٍ فِي وَقْتٍ مَخْصُوصٍ.

---

[32] Recorded by Muslim (588) from Aboo Hurayrah ﷺ.

[33] Recorded by Muslim (728) from Umm Habeebah ﷺ.

[34] [TN] The *Sunnah Rawaatib* prayers are those voluntary prayers which the Messenger of Allah ﷺ did not leave performing.

[35] [TN] That group must be from the eight groups mentioned in *Soorat-ut-Tawbah* (9):60.

50 - Define Fasting?

Answer: It is worship to Allah the Most High by refraining from breaking the fast from the break of dawn until the setting of the sun, with the intention (of worshipping Allah by it).

٥٠ – عَرِّفِ الصِّيَامَ؟

الْجَوَابُ: هُوَ التَّعَبُّدُ لله تَعَالَى بِالإِمْسَاكِ عَنْ الْمُفَطِّرَاتِ مِنْ طُلُوعِ الْفَجْرِ إِلَى غُرُوبِ الشَّمْسِ مَعَ النِّيَّةِ.

51 – Complete the (following) *Hadeeth*: The Messenger of Allah ﷺ said: "*Whoever fasts (the entire month of) Ramadaan...*"
Answer: "*...out of Imaan and hope (for reward from Allah), whatever (minor) sins he previously did are forgiven.*"(36)

٥١ – أَكْمِلِ الْحَدِيثَ... قَالَ رَسُولُ الله ﷺ: ((مَنْ صَامَ رَمَضَانَ...؟

الْجَوَابُ: ...إِيمَانًا وَاحْتِسَابًا غُفِرَ لَهُ مَا تَقَدَّمَ مِنْ ذَنْبِهِ)).

52 – Define *Hajj*?

Answer: It is worship to Allah the Most High with the intention (of making *Hajj*) at His Sacred House (the Ka'bah) with specific actions during a specific time(37).

٥٢ – عَرِّفِ الْحَجَّ؟

الْجَوَابُ: هُوَ التَّعَبُّدُ لله تَعَالَى بِقَصْدِ بَيْتِهِ الْحَرَامِ لأَعْمَالٍ مَخْصُوصَةٍ فِي زَمَنٍ مَخْصُوصٍ.

53 – Complete the (following) *Hadeeth*: The Messenger of Allah ﷺ said: "*Whoever carries out Hajj for Allah (alone) and does not use obscene speech and does not do anything evil...*"

٥٣ – أَكْمِلِ الْحَدِيثَ... قَالَ رَسُولُ الله ﷺ: ((مَنْ حَجَّ لله وَلَمْ يَرْفُثْ وَلَمْ يَفْسُقْ...؟

---

(36) Recorded by Al-Bukhaaree (38) and Muslim (760) from Aboo Hurayrah ﷺ.
(37) [TN] i.e. During the months of *Hajj*: *Shawwaal, Dhul-Qa'dah* and *Dhul-Hijjah*.

Answer: "...*He will return from his sins (to a state) like the day his mother gave birth to him (i.e. his minor sins will be forgiven).*"[38]

الْجَوَابُ: ...رَجَعَ مِنْ ذَنْبِهِ كَيَوْمٍ وَلَدَتْهُ أُمُّهُ)).

54 – What are the pillars of *Imaan*[39]?
Answer:

1) *Imaan* in Allah;

2) and His Angels;

3) and His Books;

4) and His Messengers;

5) and the Last Day;

6) and *Qadr*[40]; its good and evil, are from Allah the Most High.

٤٥ – مَا أَرْكَانُ الْإِيمَانِ؟

الْجَوَابُ:

(١) الْإِيمَانُ بِاللهِ.

(٢) وَمَلَائِكَتِهِ.

(٣) وَكُتُبِهِ.

(٤) وَرُسُلِهِ.

(٥) وَالْيَوْمِ الْآخِرِ.

(٦) وَالْقَدَرِ خَيْرِهِ وَشَرِّهِ مِنَ اللهِ تَعَالَى.

55 – Mention three names from the Angels?
Answer: Jibreel, Meekaa'eel and Israafeel.

٥٥ – اُذْكُرْ أَسْمَاءَ ثَلَاثَةٍ مِنَ الْمَلَائِكَةِ؟

الْجَوَابُ: جِبْرِيل، مِيكَائِيل، إِسْرَافِيل.

56 – Mention the Divine Books and who they were revealed to?

Answer:

٥٦ – اُذْكُرِ الْكُتُبَ السَّمَاوِيَّةَ وَعَلَى مَنْ نَزَلَتْ؟

الْجَوَابُ:

---

[38] Recorded by Al-Bukhaaree (1521) from Aboo Hurayrah ﷺ.

[39] *Imaan* is the faith which is uttered on the tongue, affirmed in the heart and carried out with the limbs, it increases with obedience to Allah and decreases with disobedience to Him.

[40] A Muslim cannot believe in *al-Qadr* correctly until he believes that Allah created all things, that He knew their future and fate, that He ordered the Pen to record all that would occur among the creation and that all of those things happen by the Will and Power of Allah alone.

1) The *Suhuf* (Scriptures) of Ibraaheem and Musaa (which were revelead) to our leaders Ibraaheem and Musaa (عليهما السلام).

2) The *Zaboor* which (was revealed) to our leader Dawud ﷺ.

3) The *Tawraah* which (was revealed) to our leader Musaa ﷺ.

4) The *Injeel* which (was revealed) to our leader *Eesaa* ﷺ.

5) The Noble *Qur'aan* (which was revealed) to our leader Muhammad ﷺ.

57 – Who are the *Oolul-'Azm* (strongest in determination) from the Messengers?
Answer:

1) Nooh ﷺ.
2) Ibraaheem ﷺ.
3) Moosaa ﷺ.
4) Eesaa ﷺ.
5) Muhammad ﷺ.

58 – Recite the end of *Surat-ul-Baqarah* which a Muslim recites before sleeping?(41)
Answer:

(١) صُحُفُ إِبْرَاهِيمَ وَمُوسَى عَلَى سَيِّدِنَا إِبْرَاهِيمَ وَمُوسَى عَلَيْهِمَا السَّلَامُ.

(٢) الزَّبُورُ عَلَى سَيِّدِنَا دَاوُودَ عَلَيْهِ السَّلَامُ.

(٣) التَّوْرَاةُ عَلَى سَيِّدِنَا مُوسَى عَلَيْهِ السَّلَامُ.

(٤) الإِنْجِيلُ عَلَى سَيِّدِنَا عِيسَى عَلَيْهِ لسَّلَامُ.

(٥) الْقُرْآنُ الْكَرِيمُ عَلَى سَيِّدِنَا مُحَمَّدٍ صَلَّى اللهُ عَلَيْهِ وَسَلَّمَ.

٥٧- مَنْ هُمْ أُولُو الْعَزْمِ مِنَ الرُّسُلِ؟

الْجَوَابُ:

(١) نُوحُ عَلَيْهِ لسَّلَامُ.
(٢) إِبْرَاهِيمَ عَلَيْهِ لسَّلَامُ.
(٣) مُوسَى عَلَيْهِ لسَّلَامُ.
(٤) عِيسَى عَلَيْهِ لسَّلَامُ.
(٥) مُحَمَّدٌ ﷺ.

٥٨- اِقْرَأْ خَوَاتِمَ سُورَةِ الْبَقَرَةِ الَّتِي يَقْرَأُهَا الْمُسْلِمُ قَبْلَ النَّوْمِ؟

الْجَوَابُ:

---

(41) Soorat-ul-Baqarah (2):285-286,

﴿ ءَامَنَ ٱلرَّسُولُ بِمَآ أُنزِلَ إِلَيْهِ مِن رَّبِّهِۦ وَٱلْمُؤْمِنُونَ ۚ كُلٌّ ءَامَنَ بِٱللَّهِ وَمَلَٰٓئِكَتِهِۦ وَكُتُبِهِۦ وَرُسُلِهِۦ لَا نُفَرِّقُ بَيْنَ أَحَدٍ مِّن رُّسُلِهِۦ ۚ وَقَالُوا۟ سَمِعْنَا وَأَطَعْنَا ۖ غُفْرَانَكَ رَبَّنَا وَإِلَيْكَ ٱلْمَصِيرُ. لَا يُكَلِّفُ ٱللَّهُ نَفْسًا إِلَّا وُسْعَهَا ۚ لَهَا مَا كَسَبَتْ وَعَلَيْهَا مَا ٱكْتَسَبَتْ ۗ رَبَّنَا لَا تُؤَاخِذْنَآ إِن نَّسِينَآ أَوْ أَخْطَأْنَا ۚ رَبَّنَا وَلَا تَحْمِلْ عَلَيْنَآ إِصْرًا كَمَا حَمَلْتَهُۥ عَلَى ٱلَّذِينَ مِن قَبْلِنَا ۚ رَبَّنَا وَلَا تُحَمِّلْنَا مَا لَا طَاقَةَ لَنَا بِهِۦ ۖ وَٱعْفُ عَنَّا وَٱغْفِرْ لَنَا وَٱرْحَمْنَآ ۚ أَنتَ مَوْلَىٰنَا فَٱنصُرْنَا عَلَى ٱلْقَوْمِ ٱلْكَٰفِرِينَ. ﴾

"(285) The Messenger believes in what has been sent down to him from his Rabb, as (do) the believers; each one believes in Allah, His Angels, His Books, and His Messengers; they say: "We make no distinction between any of His Messengers"; and they say: "We hear, and we obey. (We seek) Your Forgiveness, our Rabb, and to You is the return (of all). (286) Allah does not burden a person beyond his ability. He gets reward for that (good) which he has earned, and he is punished for that (evil) which he has earned. "Our Rabb! Do not punish us if we forget or fall into error; Our Rabb! Do not put on us a burden like that which you put on those before us (the Jews and Christians); Our Rabb! Do not put on us a burden greater than we have strength to bear. Pardon us and grant us Forgiveness. Have Mercy on us. You are our Protector, and give us victory over the disbelieving people.""

59 – When is the Hour (the Day of Judgement) going to be established?
Answer: Its knowledge is with Allah, nobody knows it except Him.

٥٩ – مَتَى تَقُومُ السَّاعَةُ؟
الْجَوَابُ: عِلْمُهَا عِنْدَ اللهِ لَا يَعْلَمُهَا إِلَّا هُوَ.

60 – What is the *Daarul Karaamah (Abode of Honour)*?
Answer: Al-Jannah.

٦٠ – مَا دَارُ الْكَرَامَةِ؟
الْجَوَابُ: الْجَنَّةُ.

61 – How many number of gates does *Jannah* have?

Answer: Eight gates.

٦١ – كَمْ عَدَدُ أَبْوَابِ الْجَنَّةِ؟

الْجَوَابُ: ثَمَانِيَةُ أَبْوَابٍ.

62 – When will the believers see their *Rabb*?

Answer: When they enter *Jannah*.

٦٢ – مَتَى يَرَى الْمُؤْمِنُونَ رَبَّهُم؟

الْجَوَابُ: إِذَا دَخَلُوا الْجَنَّةَ.

63 – What are the major causes which enter one into *Jannah*?

Answer: *Taqwaa*[42] of Allah and good manners.

٦٣ – مَا أَكْثَرُ مَا يُدْخِلُ الْجَنَّةَ؟

الْجَوَابُ: تَقْوَى اللهِ وَحُسْنُ الْخُلُقِ.

64 – What is the '*place of punishment and disgrace*'?

Answer: The Fire.

٦٤ – مَا دَارُ الْعَذَابِ وَالْمُهَانَةِ؟

الْجَوَابُ: النَّارُ.

65 – How many number of gates does the Fire have?

Answer: Seven gates.

٦٥ – كَمْ عَدَدَ أَبْوَابِ النَّارِ؟

الْجَوَابُ: سَبْعَةُ أَبْوَابٍ.

66 – What is *Ihsaan*?

Answer: That you worship Allah as though you see Him, and if you cannot (worship Him) as though you see Him, then (you remember that) He sees you.

٦٦ – مَا الإِحْسَانُ؟

الْجَوَابُ: أَنْ تَعْبُدَ اللهَ كَأَنَّكَ تَرَاهُ فَإِنْ لَمْ تَكُنْ تَرَاهُ، فَإِنَّهُ يَرَاكَ.

---

[42] [TN] *Taqwaa* is to protect oneself from Allah's anger and punishment by obeying His commands and avoiding His prohibitions.

67 – Who from mankind has the most right to your good behaviour and best treatment?

Answer: The two parents (the mother and the father).

٦٧ – مَنْ أَحَقُّ النَّاسِ بِالْبِرِّ والإِحْسَانِ؟

الْجَوَابُ: الْوَالِدَانِ (الأُمُّ وَالأَبُ).

68 – What do you say when you want to make *Du'aa* for your parents?

Answer: (I say) *"My Rabb, pardon my parents and have mercy on them both as they raised me when I was young."*

٦٨ – مَاذَا تَقُولُ إِذَا أَرَدْتَ أَنْ تَدْعُوَ لِوَالِدَيْكَ؟

الْجَوَابُ: رَبِّ اغْفِرْ لِي وَلِوَالِدَيَّ وَارْحَمْهُمَا كَمَا رَبَّيَانِي صَغِيرًا.

69 – What is the most beloved of actions to Allah?

Answer: The *Salaah* at its fixed times, then good behaviour with one's parents, then *Jihaad* in the path of Allah.

٦٩ – مَا أَحَبُّ الأَعْمَالِ إِلَى اللهِ؟

الْجَوَابُ: الصَّلاةُ عَلَى وَقْتِهَا، ثُمَّ بِرُّ الْوَالِدَيْنِ، ثُمَّ الْجِهَادُ فِي سَبِيلِ اللهِ.

70 – Who is the most noble of mankind according to Allah the Most High?

Answer: Those who have the most *Taqwaa* and the one with the most *Taqwaa* from all of mankind is the Messenger of Allah ﷺ.

٧٠ – مَنْ أَكْرَمُ النَّاسِ عِنْدَ اللهِ تَعَالَى؟

الْجَوَابُ: أَتْقَاهُمْ وَأَتْقَى النَّاسِ رَسُولُ اللهِ ﷺ.

71 – What is your great book?

Answer: The Noble Qur'aan.

٧١ – مَا كِتَابُكَ الْعَظِيمُ؟

الْجَوَابُ: الْقُرْآنُ الْكَرِيمُ.

72 – How many number of *Juzz* (parts) are in the Noble Qur'aan?

٧٢ – كَمْ عَدَدُ أَجْزَاءِ الْقُرْآنِ الْكَرِيمِ؟

Answer: Thirty *Juzz*.

الْجَوَابُ: ثَلَاثُونَ جُزْءًا.

73 – What do you do before you read the Noble Qur'aan?

٧٣ – مَاذَا تَفْعَلُ قَبْلَ أَنْ تَقْرَأَ الْقُرْآنَ الْكَرِيمَ؟

Answer: I make *Wudoo'* then I seek protection with Allah from *Shaytaan ar-rajeem*.[43]

الْجَوَابُ: أَتَوَضَّأُ ثُمَّ اسْتَعِيذُ بِاللهِ مِنَ الشَّيْطَانِ الرَّجِيمِ.

74 – What are the *Mu'awwidhataan*? And can you recite them both?

٧٤ – مَا الْمُعَوِّذَتَانِ؟ وَاقْرَأْهُمَا؟

Answer: *Soorat-ul-Falaq*[44]:

الْجَوَابُ: سُورَةُ الْفَلَقِ:

﴿ قُلْ أَعُوذُ بِرَبِّ الْفَلَقِ . مِن شَرِّ مَا خَلَقَ . وَمِن شَرِّ غَاسِقٍ إِذَا وَقَبَ . وَمِن شَرِّ النَّفَّثَتِ فِي الْعُقَدِ . وَمِن شَرِّ حَاسِدٍ إِذَا حَسَدَ ﴾

"(In the Name of Allah – Ar-Rahmaan – Ar-Raheem) (1) Say: 'I seek protection with the Rabb of the daybreak; (2) From the evil that He has created; (3) And from the evil of the darkening (night) when it comes with its darkness; (4) And from the evil of those who do witchcraft when they blow knots; (5) And from the evil of the envier when he envies.'"

And *Soorat-un-Naas*[45]:

وَسُورَةُ النَّاسِ:

﴿ قُلْ أَعُوذُ بِرَبِّ النَّاسِ . مَلِكِ النَّاسِ . إِلَهِ النَّاسِ . مِن شَرِّ الْوَسْوَاسِ

---

[43] [TN] Shaytaan (Iblees) is described as *ar-Rajeem* which means: expelled from all types of good.

[44] Al-Falaq (113):1-5

[45] An-Naas (114):1-6

ٱلْخَنَّاسِ . ٱلَّذِى يُوَسْوِسُ فِى صُدُورِ ٱلنَّاسِ . مِنَ ٱلْجِنَّةِ وَٱلنَّاسِ ﴾

"(In the Name of Allah – Ar-Rahmaan – Ar-Raheem) (1) Say: 'I seek refuge
with (Allah) the Lord of mankind, (2) The King of mankind, (3) The Ilaah
of mankind, (4) From the evil of the whisperer (devil who whispers evil in
the hearts of men) who withdraws (from his whispering in one's heart after
one remembers Allah). (5) Who whispers in the breasts of mankind. (6) Of
jinn and men.'"

75 – What is the greatest *Ayah* in
the Noble Qur'an? And can you
recite it?

٧٥ - مَا أَعْظَمُ آيَةٍ فِي الْقُرْآنِ الْكَرِيمِ؟
وَاقْرَأْهَا؟

Answer: *Aayat-ul-Kursee*[46]:

الْجَوَابُ: آيَةُ الْكُرْسِيِّ:

﴿ ٱللَّهُ لَآ إِلَٰهَ إِلَّا هُوَ ٱلْحَىُّ ٱلْقَيُّومُ ۚ لَا تَأْخُذُهُ سِنَةٌ وَلَا نَوْمٌ لَّهُ ۥ مَا فِى

ٱلسَّمَٰوَٰتِ وَمَا فِى ٱلْأَرْضِ ۗ مَن ذَا ٱلَّذِى يَشْفَعُ عِندَهُ ٓ إِلَّا بِإِذْنِهِ ۦ ۚ يَعْلَمُ مَا

بَيْنَ أَيْدِيهِمْ وَمَا خَلْفَهُمْ ۖ وَلَا يُحِيطُونَ بِشَىْءٍ مِّنْ عِلْمِهِ ٓ إِلَّا بِمَا شَآءَ ۚ

وَسِعَ كُرْسِيُّهُ ٱلسَّمَٰوَٰتِ وَٱلْأَرْضَ ۖ وَلَا يَـُٔودُهُ حِفْظُهُمَا ۚ وَهُوَ ٱلْعَلِىُّ ٱلْعَظِيمُ ﴾

"Allah, there is nothing deserving of worship except Him, the Ever-Living,
the Ever-Sustaining; drowsiness and sleep does not overtake Him; to Him
belongs all things in the heavens and on earth; who can intercede with Him
except by His permission? He knows what happens to His creation in this
world and what will happen to them in the Hereafter; and they will never
cover anything of His knowledge except what He wills; His Kursee
(footstool) stretches over the heavens and the earth, and He feels no
tiredness in preserving them; and He is the Most High, the Most Great."

76 – Complete the (following)
Hadeeth: The Messenger of Allah ﷺ

٧٦ - أَكْمِلِ الْحَدِيثَ... قَالَ رَسُولُ اللهِ

---

[46] Al-Baqarah (2):255

said: "*Whoever recites Ayaat-ul-Kursee after completing every Salaah...*"

Answer: "*...nothing prevents him from entering Jannah except death.*"[47]

ﷺ: ((مَنْ قَرَأَ آيَةَ الْكُرْسِيِّ دُبُرَ كُلِّ صَلاةٍ...؟

الْجَوَابُ: ...لَمْ يَمْنَعْهُ مِنْ دُخُولِ الْجَنَّةِ إِلاَّ أَنْ يَمُوتَ)).

77 – What is the best *Soorah* in the Noble Qur'aan? And can you recite it?

Answer: *Soorat-ul-Faatihah*[48]:

٧٧ – مَا أَفْضَلُ سُورَةٍ فِي الْقُرْآنِ؟ وَاقْرَأْهَا؟

الْجَوَابُ: سُورَةُ الْفَاتِحَةِ:

﴿ بِسْمِ اللَّهِ الرَّحْمَنِ الرَّحِيمِ . الْحَمْدُ لِلَّهِ رَبِّ الْعَلَمِينَ . الرَّحْمَنِ الرَّحِيمِ . مَلِكِ يَوْمِ الدِّينِ . إِيَّاكَ نَعْبُدُ وَإِيَّاكَ نَسْتَعِينُ . اهْدِنَا الصِّرَطَ الْمُسْتَقِيمَ . صِرَطَ الَّذِينَ أَنْعَمْتَ عَلَيْهِمْ غَيْرِ الْمَغْضُوبِ عَلَيْهِمْ وَلَا الضَّالِّينَ ﴾

"(1) In the Name of Allah – Ar-Rahmaan – Ar-Raheem; (2) All praise and thanks is for Allah, the Rabb of all creation; (3) Ar-Rahman – Ar-Raheem; (4) The Master of the Day of Repayment; (5) You (alone) we worship and You (alone) we ask for help; (6) Guide us to the straight path; (7) The path of those who You have favoured, not of those who You are angry with or those who have gone astray."

78 – What is the longest *Soorah* in the Noble Qur'aan?

Answer: *Soorat-ul-Baqarah*.

٧٨ – مَا أَطْوَلُ سُورَةٍ فِي الْقُرْآنِ الْكَرِيمِ؟

الْجَوَابُ: سُورَةُ الْبَقَرَةِ.

---

[47] Recorded by An-Nasaa'ee [in *Sunan-ul-Kubraa* (9848)] from Aboo Umaamah ﷺ. ([TN] Shaykh Al-Albaanee graded it *Saheeh* (*Silsilah*, 972).

[48] Al-Faatihah (1):1-7

79 – What is the shortest *Soorah* in the Noble Qur'an?

Answer: *Soorat-ul-Kawthar*[49]:

٧٩ – مَا أَقْصَرُ سُورَةٍ فِي الْقُرْآنِ الْكَرِيمِ؟

الْجَوَابُ: سُورَةُ الْكَوْثَرِ:

﴿ إِنَّآ أَعْطَيْنَٰكَ ٱلْكَوْثَرَ ۝ فَصَلِّ لِرَبِّكَ وَٱنْحَرْ ۝ إِنَّ شَانِئَكَ هُوَ ٱلْأَبْتَرُ ۝ ﴾

(In the Name of Allah – Ar-Rahmaan – Ar-Raheem) "(1) Verily, We have granted you *al-Kawthar* (a river in Jannah); (2) So turn in *Salah* to your *Rabb* and sacrifice (to Him alone); (3) For he who makes you angry will be cut off (from all good)."

80 – What is the *Soorah* which is equivalent to one-third of the Qur'aan?

Answer: *Soorat-ul-Ikhlaas*[50]:

٨٠ – مَا السُّورَةُ الَّتِي تَعْدِلُ ثُلُثَ الْقُرْآنِ؟

الْجَوَابُ: سُورَةُ الْإِخْلَاصِ:

﴿ قُلْ هُوَ ٱللَّهُ أَحَدٌ . ٱللَّهُ ٱلصَّمَدُ . لَمْ يَلِدْ وَلَمْ يُولَدْ . وَلَمْ يَكُن لَّهُ كُفُوًا أَحَدٌ ﴾

(In the Name of Allah – Ar-Rahmaan – Ar-Raheem) "(1) Say: 'He is Allah, the One; (2) Allah the Self-Sufficient; (3) He has no children and He has no parents; (4) And there is absolutely nothing like Him.'"

81 – Complete the (following) *Soorah*: In the Name of Allah – Ar-Rahmaan – Ar-Raheem. "(1) By Time; (2) All of mankind is in loss..."

Answer: "...(3) Except those who have Imaan and do righteous actions; and

٨١ – أَكْمِلِ السُّورَةَ: بِسْمِ اللهِ الرَّحْمَٰنِ الرَّحِيمِ .

﴿ وَٱلْعَصْرِ إِنَّ ٱلْإِنسَٰنَ لَفِى خُسْرٍ... ؟

الْجَوَابُ: ...إِلَّا ٱلَّذِينَ ءَامَنُوا۟ وَعَمِلُوا۟

---

[49] Al-Kawthar (108):1-3
[50] Al-Ikhlaas (112):1-4

encourage each other to the truth and
encourage each other to practise
patience."[51]

الصَّالِحَاتِ وَتَوَاصَوْا بِالْحَقِّ وَتَوَاصَوْا
بِالصَّبْرِ﴾

82 – What is the best characteristic
and is the most virtuous?
Answer: Truthfulness.

٨٢ – مَا أَحْسَنُ الأَخْلاقِ وَأَفْضَلُهَا؟
الْجَوَابُ: الصِّدْقُ.

83 – What is the ugliest
characteristic and is the most evil?
Answer: Lying.

٨٣ – مَا أَقْبَحُ الأَخْلاقِ وَأَسْوَؤُهَا؟
الْجَوَابُ: الْكَذِبُ.

84 – Complete the (following)
Hadeeth: The Messenger of Allah ﷺ
said: "None of you will (truly) believe
until he loves..."
Answer: "...for his brother what he
loves for himself."[52]

٨٤ – أَكْمِلِ الْحَدِيثَ... قَالَ رَسُولُ الله
ﷺ: ((لا يُؤْمِنُ أَحَدُكُمْ حَتَّى يُحِبَّ...؟
الْجَوَابُ: ...لأَخِيهِ مَا يُحِبُّ لِنَفْسِهِ)).

85 – Who is your enemy?

Answer: Shaytaan Ar-Rajeem.

٨٥ – مَنْ عَدُوُّكَ؟
الْجَوَابُ: الشَّيْطَانُ الرَّجِيمُ.

86 – When do you seek protection
with Allah from Shaytaan Ar-
Rajeem?
Answer:

1) Before reading the Qur'an.

2) Before entering the toilet area.

3) When getting angry.

٨٦ – مَتَى تَسْتَعِيذُ بِالله مِنَ الشَّيْطَانِ
الرَّجِيمِ؟
الْجَوَابُ:
(١) قَبْلَ قِرَاءَةِ الْقُرْآنِ.
(٢) قَبْلَ دُخُولِ الْخَلاءِ.

---

[51] Al-'Asr (103):1-3
[52] Recorded by Al-Bukhaaree (13) and Muslim (45) from Anas bin Maalik ﷺ.

4) When getting *waswasah* (evil whispers from *Shaytan*).

5) When hearing the braying of the donkey.

(٣) عِنْدَ الْغَضَبِ.

(٤) عِنْدَ الْوَسْوَسَةِ.

(٥) عِنْدَ سَمَاعِ نَهِيقِ الْحِمَارِ.

87 – What is the most dangerous disease of the heart?

Answer: *Nifaaq* (hypocrisy).

٨٧ – مَا أَخْطَرُ أَمْرَاضِ الْقُلُوبِ؟

الْجَوَابُ: النِّفَاقُ.

88 – What is the heaviest *Salaah* upon the hypocrites?

Answer: *Fajr Salaah* and *Ishaa'a Salaah.*

٨٨ – مَا أَثْقَلُ الصَّلَاةِ عَلَى الْمُنَافِقِينَ؟

الْجَوَابُ: صَلَاةُ الصُّبْحِ وَالْعِشَاءِ.

89 – Complete the (following) *Hadeeth*: The Messenger of Allah ﷺ said: "*The signs of the hypocrite are three: (1) when he speaks, he lies...*"

Answer: "*...(2) when he makes a promise, he breaks it, (3) and when he is trusted, he betrays (that trust).*"[53]

٨٩ – أَكْمِلِ الْحَدِيثَ... قَالَ رَسُولُ اللهِ ﷺ: ((آيَةُ الْمُنَافِقِ ثَلَاثٌ: إِذَا حَدَّثَ كَذَبَ...؟

الْجَوَابُ: ...وَإِذَا وَعَدَ أَخْلَفَ وَإِذَا اتُّمِنَ خَانَ.((

90 – What is the most dangerous thing upon mankind?

Answer: The tongue (when it is used to say or spread evil).

٩٠ – مَا أَخْطَرُ شَيْءٍ عَلَى الْإِنْسَانِ؟

الْجَوَابُ: اللِّسَانُ.

91 – Complete the (following) *Hadeeth*: The Messenger of Allah ﷺ said: "*From the best of a man's*

٩١ – أَكْمِلِ الْحَدِيثَ... قَالَ رَسُولُ اللهِ ﷺ: ((مِنْ حُسْنِ إِسْلَامِ الْمَرْءِ...؟

---

[53] Recorded by Al-Bukhaaree (33) and Muslim (59) from Aboo Hurayrah ⬥.

(practise of) Islam is..."
Answer: "...that he leaves that which
does not concern him."(54)

الْجَوَابُ: ...تَرْكُهُ مَا لَا يَعْنِيهِ)).

92 – What is the most beloved
statement to Allah the Most High?
Answer: *Allah is free from all types of
imperfections, all praise and thanks is
for Allah, and there is nothing that
deserves to be worshipped except Allah
and Allah is the most Great.*

٩٢ – مَا أَحَبُّ الْكَلَامِ إِلَى اللهِ تَعَالَى؟

الْجَوَابُ: سُبْحَانَ اللهِ، وَالْحَمْدُ لله، وَلَا إِلَهَ
إِلَّا اللهُ، وَاللهُ أَكْبَرُ.

93 – What is the treasure of
Jannah?
Answer: *There is no movement or
power except by (the permission of)
Allah.*

٩٣ – مَا كَنْزُ الْجَنَّةِ؟

الْجَوَابُ: لَا حَوْلَ وَلَا قُوَّةَ إِلَّا بِاللهِ.

94 – Complete the (following)
Hadeeth: The Messenger of Allah ﷺ
said: "*There are two statements
which are light on the tongue...*"
Answer: "*...heavy on the scales, beloved
to Ar-Rahmaan, (they are): Allah is free
from all types of imperfections and all
praise is for Him, Allah is free from all
types of imperfections the Most Great.*"
(55)

٩٤ – أَكْمِلِ الْحَدِيثَ... قَال رَسُولُ اللهِ
ﷺ: ((كَلِمَتَانِ خَفِيفَتَانِ عَلَى اللِّسَانِ...؟

الْجَوَابُ: ...ثَقِيلَتَانِ فِي الْمِيزَانِ، حَبِيبَتَانِ
إِلَى الرَّحْمَنِ: سُبْحَانَ اللهِ وَبِحَمْدِهِ، سُبْحَانَ
اللهِ الْعَظِيمِ)).

95 – Mention the *sayyid-ul-
istighfaar (the best way of seeking
forgiveness from Allah)?*

٩٥ – اذْكُرْ سَيِّدَ الِاسْتِغْفَارِ؟

---

(54) Recorded by At-Tirmidhee (2317) and Ibn Maajah (3976) from Aboo Hurayrah ﷺ.
(55) Recorded by Al-Bukhaaree (7563) and Muslim (2694) from Aboo Hurayrah ﷺ.

Answer: The *sayyid-ul-istighfaar* is that the slave (of Allah) says: "*O Allah! My Rabb, none deserves to be worshipped but You, You created me and I am Your slave, and I am upon Your covenant and Your promise according to what I am able, I seek protection from the evil of what I have done and I recognise Your favours upon me, and I recognise before You my sins, so forgive me for no one can forgive sins except You.*"[56]

الْجَوَابُ: سَيِّدُ الِاسْتِغْفَارِ أَنْ يَقُولَ الْعَبْدُ: (اللَّهُمَّ أَنْتَ رَبِّي لَا إِلَهَ إِلَّا أَنْتَ، خَلَقْتَنِي وَأَنَا عَبْدُكَ وَأَنَا عَلَى عَهْدِكَ وَوَعْدِكَ مَا اسْتَطَعْتُ، أَعُوذُ بِكَ مِنْ شَرِّ مَا صَنَعْتُ وَأَبُوءُ لَكَ بِنِعْمَتِكَ عَلَيَّ وَأَبُوءُ لَكَ بِذَنْبِي فَاغْفِرْ لِي فَإِنَّهُ لَا يَغْفِرُ الذُّنُوبَ إِلَّا أَنْتَ).

96 – What do you say before sleeping?
Answer: "*With Your Name O Allah I die and I live.*"[57]

٩٦ – مَا تَقُولُ قَبْلَ النَّوْمِ؟
الْجَوَابُ: بِاسْمِكَ اللَّهُمَّ أَمُوتُ وَأَحْيَا.

97 – What do you say after you wake up from sleep?
Answer: All praise and thanks is for Allah who gave us life after death and to You (O Allah) is the return.[58]

٩٧ – مَا تَقُولُ بَعْدَ الِاسْتِيقَاظِ مِنَ النَّوْمِ؟
الْجَوَابُ: الْحَمْدُ لله الَّذِي أَحْيَانَا بَعْدَ مَا أَمَاتَنَا وَإِلَيْهِ النُّشُورُ.

98 – What is the greeting of Islam?
Answer: *Peace be upon you and the mercy of Allah and His blessings.*

٩٨ – مَا تَحِيَّةُ الْإِسْلَامِ؟
الْجَوَابُ: السَّلَامُ عَلَيْكُمْ وَرَحْمَةُ الله وَبَرَكَاتُهُ.

99 – Which of the two hands does the Muslim eat and drink with?
Answer: With the right hand.

٩٩ – بِأَيِّ الْيَدَيْنِ يَأْكُلُ وَيَشْرَبُ الْمُسْلِمُ؟
الْجَوَابُ: بِالْيَدِ الْيُمْنَى.

---

[56] Recorded by Al-Bukhaaree (6306) from Shaddaad bin Aws ﷺ.

[57] [TN] As is stated in a *Hadeeth* recorded by Al-Bukhaaree (6324) from Hudhayfah ﷺ.

[58] [TN] As is stated in a *Hadeeth* recorded by Muslim (2711) from Al-Baraa' ﷺ.

100 – When do you say: *Bismillah* (in the name of Allah)?
Answer:

1) Before eating and drinking.
2) Before entering the toilet area.
3) Before entering the *Masjid*.
4) After leaving from it (the *Masjid*).
5) Before removing clothes.

١٠٠ – مَتَى تَقُولُ (بِسْمِ اللهِ)؟

الْجَوَابُ:

(١) قَبْلَ الأَكْلِ وَالشَّرْبِ.

(٢) قَبْلَ دُخُولِ الْخَلَاءِ.

(٣) قَبْلَ دُخُولِ الْمَسْجِدِ.

(٤) بَعْدَ الْخُرُوجِ مِنْهُ.

(٥) قَبْلَ خَلْعِ الْمَلَابِسَ.

101 – When do you say: All praise and thanks for Allah?
Answer:

1) After eating and drinking.
2) After sneezing.
3) After every favour.
4) In every condition.

١٠١ – مَتَى تَقُولُ الْحَمْدُ لله؟

الْجَوَابُ:

(١) بَعْدَ الأَكْلِ وَالشَّرْبِ.

(٢) بَعْدَ الْعُطَاسِ.

(٣) بَعْدَ كُلِّ نِعْمَةٍ.

(٤) فِي كُلِّ حَالٍ.

102 – What do you say to the one who sneezes and (then) praises Allah?
Answer: *May Allah have mercy upon you.*

١٠٢ – مَاذَا تَقُولُ لِمَنْ عَطَسَ وَحَمِدَ الله؟

الْجَوَابُ: (يَرْحَمُكَ الله).

103 – What do you say to the one who says to you: "*May Allah have mercy upon you*," after (you) sneeze (and praise Allah)?

١٠٣ – مَاذَا تَقُولُ لِمَنْ قَالَ لَكَ يَرْحَمُكَ الله بَعْدَ الْعُطَاسِ؟

Answer: *May Allah guide you and correct your affairs.*

الْجَوَابُ: يَهْدِيكُمُ اللهُ وَيُصْلِحُ بَالَكُمْ.

104 – Complete the (following) *Hadeeth:* The Messenger of Allah ﷺ said: "*Whoever Allah desires good for...*"?

Answer: "*...He gives him (correct) understanding of the Deen.*" [59]

١٠٤ - أَكْمِلِ الْحَدِيثَ... قَالَ رَسُولُ اللهِ ﷺ: ((مَنْ يُرِدِ اللهُ بِهِ خَيْرًا...؟

الْجَوَابُ: ...يُفَقِّهْهُ فِي الدِّينِ)).

105 – What is the most beloved of places to Allah?

Answer: The *Masjids.*

١٠٥ - مَا أَحَبُّ الْأَمَاكِنِ إِلَى اللهِ؟

الْجَوَابُ: الْمَسَاجِدُ.

106 – What is the best day of the week?

Answer: The day of *Jum'ah (Friday).*

١٠٦ - مَا أَفْضَلُ أَيَّامِ الْأُسْبُوعِ؟

الْجَوَابُ: يَوْمُ الْجُمْعَةِ.

107 – What is the best day in the year?

Answer: The day of *Arafah (the 9th of Dhul-Hijjah).*

١٠٧ - مَا أَفْضَلُ يَوْمٍ فِي الْعَامِ؟

الْجَوَابُ: يَوْمُ عَرَفَةَ.

108 – What is the best night in the year?

Answer: The night of *Al-Qadr.*

١٠٨ - مَا أَفْضَلُ لَيْلَةٍ فِي الْعَامِ؟

الْجَوَابُ: لَيْلَةُ الْقَدْرِ.

109 – What is the best of months?

Answer: The month of *Ramadhaan.*

١٠٩ - مَا أَفْضَلُ الشُّهُورِ؟

الْجَوَابُ: شَهْرُ رَمَضَانَ.

---

[59] Recorded by Al-Bukhaaree (7312) and Muslim (1037) from Mu'aawiyah ﷺ.

110 – What are the Islamic days of celebration?

Answer: '*Eed-ul-Fitr* and '*Eed-ul-Ad`haa*.

١١٠ – مَا أَعْيَادُ الإِسْلَامِ؟

الْجَوَابُ: عِيدُ الْفِطْرِ وَعِيدُ الأَضْحَى.

111 – Who are the *Khulafaa-ur-Raashidoon (the rightly guided Rulers)*?

Answer:

1) Abu Bakr *as-Siddeeq*.

2) 'Umar bin Al-Khattaab.

3) 'Uthmaan bin Affaan.

4) 'Alee bin Abee Taalib .

١١١ – مَنْ هُمُ الْخُلَفَاءُ الرَّاشِدُونَ؟

الْجَوَابُ:

(١) أَبُو بَكْرٍ الصِّدِّيقِ.

(٢) عُمَرُ بْنُ الْخَطَّابِ.

(٣) عُثْمَانُ بْنُ عَفَّانٍ.

(٤) عَلِيُّ بْنُ أَبِي طَالِبٍ رضي الله عنهم أَجْمَعِينَ.

تَمَّتِ الأَسْئِلَةُ وَالأَجْوِبَةُ عَلَيْهَا،

وَالْحَمْدُ للهِ أَوَّلاً وَآخِرًا

The questions and answers to them are complete;
And all praise and thanks is due to Allah,
In the beginning and end.[60]

---

[60] [TN] And the translation of this book began and was completed during the middle of *Ramadhaan* 1428, and all praise and thanks is due to Allah ﷻ.

Notes:

Notes:

Notes:

20999784R00025

Printed in Poland
by Amazon Fulfillment
Poland Sp. z o.o., Wrocław